Nothing but Love

For You.

Poetry By
Nicola Amadora PhD.

Nothing but Love
Author: Nicola Amadora PhD.

First Edition: 2009
Second Edition 2014

Independent Publisher
ISBN 978-1494382292

1. Poetry 2. Spirituality 3. Relationship

Printed in the USA

© 2009 and 2014 by Amadora
All rights reserved.

Nothing But Love

1. Prologue..................................Page 6
2. The Feast................................Page 7
3. Tonight..................................Page 8-9
4. Dear One................................Page 10
5. Beautiful One..........................Page 11-12
6. The Last Word.........................Page 13-15
7. Welcome.................................Page 16
8. Love no matter what................Page 17-18
9. Agape's Script........................Page 19-20
10. Love is Merciless....................Page 21-22
11. Veils Departing.......................Page 23-24
12. All of It..................................Page 25
13. Light and Dark........................Page 26
14. Mirror on the Wall...................Page 27
15. Biting Softly...........................Page 28
16. Look, Traveler.........................Page 29
17. Let Stories Fall........................Page 30-31
18. Attachment.............................Page 30
19. Truth.....................................Page 33
20. Just Searching........................Page 34-35
21. Treasure This One!..................Page 36
22. Surrender..............................Page 37
23. What is Movement For?............Page 38-39
24. Silence..................................Page 40
25. Just Ok.................................Page 41
26. Luminous..............................Page 42
27. Armored...............................Page 43

28. Divine Madness..................................Page 44
29. What is this Fuss?.............................Page 45
30. Loneliness......................................Page 46
31. Grace..Page 47
32. Sleepless Night in Love....................Page 48-51
33. Compassion...................................Page 52-53
34. Spiritual Talk.................................Page 54
35. Be Here..Page 55
36. Meeting in Union...........................Page 56-57
37. Wounded......................................Page 58
38. Yes, There is Suffering....................Page 59-60
39. The Buddha Smiles.........................Page 61
40. Being Here For You ....Page 62-63
41. Why?...Page 64-65
42. If Only I Could Tell You..................Page 66-67
43. God's Orchestra.............................Page 68
44. Happiness....................................Page 69-70
45. Falling in Love...............................Page 71
46. Don't Hold Back Love....................Page 72
47. Behold...Page 73-74
48. Love is..Page 75-76
49. The Lotus grows from the mud........Page 77-79
50. True Love....................................Page 80-81
51. Be brave.....................................Page 82-85
52. Noble Man..................................Page 86-87
53. This Pain....................................Page 88-89
54. One Drop...................................Page 90
55. Come near..................................Page 91-92
56. Thou hast kept Thy promise............Page 93-94

57. I AM...Page 95-96
58. This precious earth...............................Page 97
59. Death in autumn................................Page 98-99
60. Winter solstice.....................................Page 100
61. To all who have shut down............Page 101-104
62. Your Song..Page 105
63. Yearning..Page 106
64. The naked heart.................................Page 107
65. An Offering...Page 109
66. I come for you...............................Page 110-111
67. Don't wait for love.............................Page 112
68. My love...Page 113-115
69. We..Page 116
70. Beloved...Page 117-118
71. An answer to the world's suffering
....Page 119-121
72. She..Page 122-124
73. Down from the throne.......................Page 125
74. Amore te-Let me love you............Page 126-127
75. Epilogue..Page 128-129

PROLOGUE

"Nothing but Love" is gratefully dedicated to my beautiful daughter Yemaya, my father who always believed in my talent for writing, beloved friends who held my hand, those who helped me to heal, teachers who supported my awakening and to the Mystery itself.

The poems were born from my most intimate and direct experiences, whilst going through an intense fire in my life. There was nothing left or to hold unto, but to take this amazing and at first frightening plunge into the Source of Love.

May the words touch you, open a closed door into the heart, bring balm to an aching wound and tickle you to awaken ever deeper into who you truly are and take you into the joy of meeting in love. May these poems be treasures for your daily life and inspire you to live real love with each other on this beautiful earth.

It is my honor to take your hand and my hope to be a light upon your unique path home. May my simple offering of love be of benefit to all beings.

THE FEAST

The feast is here.
Come and eat!
How long will it take you
To join us at this holy
Table of Love?
Where the wine of God
Intoxicates all of us,
Each sip filled with
Eternity's gaze and
Creation's blood?

Leave nothing out.
Get drunk in your surrender!
For the Beloved
Will have only
The Whole
Of you!

TONIGHT

Tonight
The ocean

Is shimmering
In moonlight.

Her waves
Are falling into the shore.

"Merge"

Is the ancient call,
Resounding from
The beginning of time.

Dive into this
Ocean of Love.

Come, friend.
What use is it
To stand
On some safe shore,
Longing and so afraid?

Get naked and empty.
Finally strip off all your clothes.
Dare
For once in your life
To take the leap!
Love will take you,
Make you, and drown you
To surrender
All the way.

For what will be left of you then,
My dear,
Is only this—
The jewel
Beyond price.

DEAR ONE

You have come!
Hallelujah!
Tumbled down
From heaven
Onto earth.
Painful and beautiful,
This birth.

Why not
Just be human?
Simply here,
With all that is.
Daring to experience
Joy, grief, tears, and bliss,
All One
In this ever-changing
Universe.
All met with a Yes,
Accepted in openness.

Such unfolds
Your innocence,
Like petals of a lotus flower
In the light of early morning sun,
Into a fountain
Of Love
That always is.

BEAUTIFUL ONE

I wish
I could take your hand
And make you stop running
In endless circles,
Searching in other
People's pockets
For a lost gem
And breadcrumbs of kindness
So you would finally feel loved.
Shooting arrow after arrow
To achieve goals in some far distance
So you could feel worthy
After all these years.

Sweet one, listen:
Let yourself rest
Upon warm earth,
Just for this moment,
From such hopeless endeavors.
Turn to yourself.
Let one hand
Caress the other.
Who is touching,
In such tenderness?

*Look into the mirror
To see your very own eyes,
Where the light
Of Beyond shines through,
And speak
As only Lovers do:
"Beloved one,
How could I have forsaken you?
I missed you,
Searched everywhere
In this whole wide world,
And all the time,
Beautiful One,
You were waiting,
Always here."*

*A kiss, then,
Is the beginning
Of a lifelong love story
That truly
Will never
End.*

THE LAST WORD

*Stop escaping
Anything,*

*For the Love
You are seeking*

*Is the One
You are.*

*Love so intimately
All that arrives at your door.
Dance with joy
On your living room floor.
Kiss the pain
When it takes over
Every corner of your house.
Let yourself be alive
In this gorgeous body of yours!
Let your hair down.
Cry,
And laugh some more!*

When Love moves in,
Give in.
Let it do with you
The most ordinary,
The most outrageous thing.

Just know,
Blessed friend,
Love has her own way,
And always
Has the last word
In the end.

WELCOME

You are welcome here
On this holy ground,
Where God rules every affair

Your weapons
Of defense and attack,
Which bring tears and blood—
These, you must leave at the door

Then step across
The threshold
Without the armor
Of the covered fear you bear

Only naked
And in humble dignity
May you enter
The sanctuary
Of the heart,
Where there is a feast to share

Offer a dish of delight
Unto the table of God
And enjoy
The sweet company
Of true and Love-drunk friends
Who make their home here.

LOVE, NO MATTER WHAT

Love, no matter what.
All the way through.
Meet with courage
Storms and challenges
That strengthen you.
Rise in heavenly glories
And gentle winds
That lift your soul.

Love, no matter what,
Whether you are crowned and
praised
By cheering crowds
Or stoned and hanged
On this world's cross.

Love, no matter what,
Through gain and loss
In this life's play,
For Love will make you shine.
You are that blazing light
In which no shadow can exist,
And Truth just is

Love, no matter what,
For no reason

But for the sake of Love.

Your heart is big enough!

PS:

*As a kiss reveals
a most precious gift
Hold nothing back,
For loving sets you free
At last.*

*And because of you
The world is a far better place.*

AGAPE'S SCRIPT

Love writes her own script.
Some words leave the pages,
Refuse to stay, and fall.
Agape follows no rules
But her own.
She gives you
No guarantees
As she gently strokes
Your bewildered hair,
No recipe to cook
Your own stew from.

And just when you
Have figured it all out
And seem to be on top of things,
With a smile
She pulls the rug out
From under your feet.

Let go of the railings,
Dear one,
And sink into her arms.
She's got you anyway,
Ever since you were born,
And long before, too.

Come, join this party
Where Love loves
Sinners and holy ones alike.
No difference to her—
You are one of them

Welcome here!

LOVE IS MERCILESS

Love is merciless,
Or so it may appear.
She drags you by the hair
Into her blazing fire,
Violates all your cherished beliefs,
And ruins
Your made-up card house,
Takes away everything
You hold dear,
Gives no security or promises
For a better afterlife.

When She comes,
She is here in full,
And may frighten you,
Even though you wanted Her.
She'll tear away
All your masks
And the walls you have built
To protect yourself,
Strip you empty
Until you stand naked
With your raw heart—

And then,
In her most loving
Embrace,

*She will draw
The sword
To kill you,
Too.*

*Are you ready
To die into her?*

*Then, my dear,
There is no shore
But the ocean,*

*Where you won't swim
But be drowned
In nothing*

But this Love.

VEILS DEPARTING

He draws the veils
From your beautiful face
As only a Lover will do.
There is nowhere to hide.
He is seeing you
Through all the games
You have played so well,
With such ardor,
Conviction, and pretense,
You almost believed them yourself.

Loosen the grip
You hold so tight,
As if your life depends on it.
Let Him draw open
The veils by which
You are blinded.
Let it all fall,
And stand
In the glory
Of mystery and
Your plain nakedness.

He comes near,
And draws you so close
It may take your breath away.
There is nothing in you to resist
His passionate kiss
Upon your tender lips.

He will set your heart
On fire
With a Love
    that
    has
    no
    word
    nor
    end.

ALL OF IT

Drink!
Get drunk
On this inexplicable
Elixir of Love.
Be courageously
Your Self.
God wants all of it!
Your beauty and your mess,
Your glory and your brokenness.
Stop hiding, faking,
And fixing.
Come out now,
For He is here
And sees right through
To the Love
That shines in you,
Embracing every part of you,
With nothing left out.

For
Only with the whole of you
Will Love ever be real, you know!

LIGHT AND DARK

Soft breezes,
Sound of ocean waves
Crossing the shore.

Relaxing into this
Luscious body,
Simply being here.

Clouds disappear,
The sun bursts through.
Is it not often like this?

When the Light shines,
We remember
Who we really are.
When darkness fills the sky
And thunder roars,
We recoil like children
In fear.

If only your eyes
Would open all the way,
You'd see
In this whole display
There is really nothing
But Love here.
All else is just empty air!

MIRROR ON THE WALL

Every morning
You look
In the familiar mirror
And see the masks
You wear,
Some ugly, some alluring,
To cover
Your
Precious
Face.

One day,
Confused and bewildered,
You may ask:
"Who am I?"

Ah, sweet one,
Are you still having fun?

Just don't forget,
In the masquerade,
That the one
Who is looking
Is the One
You are.

BITING SOFTLY

Love
So sweet

She tickles my feet
And softly bites my ear
With her delicious kiss.
She leads me astray
Into unknown paths,
Into the fire of hell
And the bliss of nirvana
    Straight
    into
    her
    fierce
    embrace.
I am
    lost
    in
    her
And she does not
Let
Go!

LOOK, TRAVELER

Look, traveler
It is like this—
Sun and Moon
Dance together
During day and night.
How can one
Be without the other?
Joy and pain
Always hold hands
Like sister and brother.
It is only you
Who tries so hard
To take them apart.
Have you succeeded yet?
I bet no,
For Lover and Beloved
Will forever
Be One!

You know.

LET STORIES FALL

Let
All
The
Stories

About yourself,
This world,
And even God

Fall away,

No matter
How convincing,
Terrible,
Or beautiful
They may be.

"What is left, then?"
You may ask.

Nothing
And
Nobody

Only
This moment
And

Who
You
Really
Are.

ATTACHMENT

So, friend,
They told you
Attachments of the heart
Are an obstacle
On your path-
To be avoided,
Transcended,
Or cut off from
As something bad.

Let me turn
The table over:
It is through them
That the Divine One
Will get you
So vulnerable
And helplessly
Onto your knees,
Until there is
No way out.

Surrender,
For then
You dance free,
In this world's play.
Not the other way round!

TRUTH

You arrived
And took everything,
Burnt down the house.
I dig around
In the ashes,
Shattered and broken.

"So, Love," I weep,
"Have you left nothing
For me?"

"Nothing!" a voice arises
Through the thunder of silence,
Enveloping sky and earth
In her mantle so great,
I cannot account for it.

There is no me,
Only Stillness,
Just that
Which is
Here.

JUST SEARCHING

What, my dear,
Are you searching for?
Seeking everywhere,
Like an addict—
"Just this taste
One more time"—
For the lost Divine.

Face it:
Nothing fills your hunger.
Nothing leaves you satisfied.

Just for once in your life,
My dear,
Be honest:
How much have you tried,
And gotten lost along the way?
For every drug, a price to pay.

You blame your desire.
Nothing wrong with that,
You just never followed
Your ravenous hunger
All the way.

Don't stop too soon,
Covering yourself with substitutes,
Wandering like a beggar
Lifetime after lifetime.

This time, go all the way.
Enter the door that is open to you now.
Dive headlong into the Source
Where Love is home,
Waiting only for you

To fill up your empty cup!

TREASURE THIS ONE!

Treasure this One,
In front of you now:
Such shining eyes
Looking into yours,
Both innocent and wise.
A mystery of God.
Human, just like you,
But with a different storyline.

Let your hand reach out
To touch
With simple kindness
From your heart,
And both of you
Will be fed
By this One Love.

SURRENDER

Surrender

Into the void

Of the great Silence.

From there,

All actions

Of Truth

Arise.

WHAT IS MOVEMENT FOR?

What are words for,
But to speak of God's beauty?
Lips moistened by
Life's delicious kiss,
Words tumbling from your soul,
Singing praises to the Beloved,
Blessing her in every face you meet,
Resounding Truth
From the depths revealed.

What is movement for,
But to let this warm body
Dance in the footsteps
Of Love?
Dancing through rivers of bliss,
Empty desert lands,
Lonely caves,
And dark hells.
Dancing in the labyrinths
Where you feel you've lost your way,
Dancing into valleys
Of laughing flowers
And wild fires,
Celebrating all the landscapes
Of this ever-changing
Life.

*Keep moving to the
Rhythm of the One
Who painted the sky tonight.*

*Let Love move you
As she will,
And enjoy the ride.*

*What freedom
To be taken over!
What relief to
To be out control,
To live in love
And shout—
A lion's roar!*

For joy.

SILENCE

What is silence for?
Do you hear
It calling,
Closer than your
Very own breath?

Come into your heart,
And follow it.
It will lead you to
Where you truly belong,
To the place where you
And the Beloved
Are One.

JUST OK

You are OK, friend,
Just as you are,
And where you are
Right now.

You may shake
Your worried head.
But anything else
Will only get you
In such painful trouble
That it will be
Hard to find
Your way home
Again.

LUMINOUS

*Dazzled by luminous light
Across colored worlds
Shimmering bright*

*Eyes like stars
Looking into
The silent midnight,
Each smiling
In One
Beautiful face
Radiating awe and innocence:
This jewel,
A treasure,
I behold in my hand.*

*Bow to THAT!
There is really nothing else.*

ARMORED

Can you still breathe,
In the armor
That covers
Your tender heart?
Your guns of anger
Are ready to shoot
At anyone
Who comes too close
Beneath your thick skin.
You figured out smartly
How to stay in control,
So afraid to be hurt,
To love and meet
With another,
In that raw heart of yours
That longs so deeply
For true communion
In Love.

DIVINE MADNESS

What is this Beloved?
I am so in Love,
I dance and sing
On the roof of my house.

My heart is breaking
All the time.
Buckets of tears
Flood the ground.
In joy or pain,
It is the same.

Am I crazy?

This love
Has no cure
For the divine madness
Of my heart.

WHAT IS THIS FUSS?

*No outer
No inner
World exists*

*No material
No spiritual
Difference here.*

There is no line.

*The mystical
And everyday life
Are one and the same.*

*What is this fuss
Really about?*

LONELINESS

Loneliness
Did hunt me down
On a dark side street in town
And held me tight.
All I wanted to do was run.
I had nowhere to hide
And nobody by my side.

Have you forgotten me,
Or have I forgotten you?
Or is it true
There is only One
Beholding the One,
And loneliness is just
Another way
To You?

GRACE

Grace opens your sleeping eyes.
Beauty lays her hand
Upon forgetfulness.

Sacredness fills silent air.
Words and deeds
Don't matter, here.
This flame,
Beyond time and space
So alive in your heart,
Is all there is!

Shine, my Love,
Shine,
And leave the rest—
For this may be
Your very last breath!

SLEEPLESS NIGHT IN LOVE

Rolling around, restless in bed,
Turning upside down
As bodies sometimes do
When missing a touch of Love.

Birds are huddled together
In a warm nest.
Even barking dogs
Are taking a rest.
Yet the sleep you crave
Is kept at bay
By incessant
"Why, and how?"
And "I should have done that!"
Such questions
From a spinning mind
So disturb a quiet night.

Meanwhile,
Love is knocking patiently
At your closed bedroom door.

You, though,
Are all alone on the floor,
Trying hard to figure out
Important things,
In this agonizing separation

That would steal sound sleep
From even a bear
During an icy winter's night.
Exhausted from every road taken
That has led nowhere,
You lie there,
Longing so deeply
For what seems not to be here.
Would you kindly take
The plugs out from your ear, my dear,
So you may hear:
Love is still knocking,
Now, ever more clear.

And your heart,
Left with no answer,
In silent despair,
Takes the chance
And calls out loud,
"Come in, whoever you are."

She enters.
Her light blinds your insanity.
You hide under the blanket.

Graciously,
She takes the papers
From the Judge's bedside table
Cataloguing all the bad things

You have ever done,
And crumples them up
In her delicate hands.
With one swift brush,
She wipes away all your defenses
As to why you aren't loved,
And should continue to live
In your own isolated prison cell.

She crawls into your bed,
And with one silken touch of
Her dolphin skin,
She strokes your rumbling fear
Into nothing but empty air.
"Oh my dear,"
She whispers
In so beautiful a voice,
"I am so glad
You let me in.
Did you hear the nightingale sing?"
"Oh," you say,
Noticing the stillness for the first time,
"I missed that."
She laughs out loud.
"You missed me
So that you could at last enjoy
That I am really here!"

You and Love hold hands
Like best friends
Who wish to never part,
And watch the fire—
Made of all those papers from Court—
Burn and warm your two hearts into one.
Shame and guilt fly out the window,
Disappear into empty space.
You snuggle into each other
With a sigh of relief.
It makes the moon relaxed,
And the cat purrs, too.

You may ask,
"How could she love me
With my hair a mess,
Such wet sweat,
And insecure like this?"
But as if she already knew,
Before doubt crept into your
Shared Holy bed,
She says, "I love you, precious one,
With your wild hair, tears dripping from
Your eyes, your happy smile,
And all the odd things you sometimes do."

*She kisses you on the nose,
But that just isn't enough.
When you are with Love,
Only one thing
Truly makes sense—
And I must confess,
At this, all creation shouts "Yes!"—
To make Love
All night long.*

*And don't worry about anything else.
With her, you'll be awake, my dear,
All the days and nights of your life,
And sleeplessness will not disturb you
As you cradle your tired head
Into the heart of God.*

*So let Love carry you
Into the greatest rest.
Oh, in Love, dear one,
Come and make your nest.
For, sure, sweet one,
You have tasted by now
What unties all the knots in your soul.*

COMPASSION

Loneliness crept into my bed.
Grief and sorrow
Seeped through the closet door.
The fire of anger
Burned high.
Fear joined the party, too—
Unannounced, of course, as usual—
And with her came
A longing
That seemed to have no end.

"Let me out!" I screamed
In silent despair.
The night was cold.
In my misery,
My head buried deep in the ground,
I did not see
That the moon was hiding her face.
I searched for the key
To stop all this nonsense.
Yet there was nothing to be found—
Only emptiness,
And no escape
From what is.

As I opened
To let it all be,

I looked around
Through my tear-stained eyes.
And where there was
No hope left to hang onto,
I heard your song
(Or was it mine?)—
So soft and clear,
Piercing through the gloom:
"Love, my sweet crushed angel,
Is big enough
To hold this entire mess."
An embrace so warm
Flooded my aching soul.

In such humility,
I found only
Compassion
For our shared
Humanness.

SPIRITUAL TALK

You, who talks
About awakening,
You escape into emptiness and bliss—
And, then, when no one is looking,
You kick a dog
And betray your best friend.
No wonder
You feel so torn,
Depressed, and split.

Stop your spiritual talk
And blaming the world
For what's not true in you.
Stop making excuses
For your own insanity
And face yourself
Just once,
For real—

And your awakening
Will dawn
As sure
As the Sun
Rises in the morning!

BE HERE

*Life's fragrance:
Filled with buzzing bees,
Blooming flowers,
Glistening sunlight
Dancing upon leaves,
Some trash and broken glass
On the roadside.
Men shout out loud
And girls whisper secrets
Into the world.*

*There is a peace
In all of this.
So still.*

*Rest
In such aliveness.
Don't hurry away
From your home*

*Or else
You miss
The whole point of simply
Being here.*

MEETING IN UNION

Friend,
Lover,
What shall I say
When all words fail,
As we meet in true Lovingness?
What could
Separate us
Or create phantom mountains
Between us now?

Nothing, really, isn't it?

As we meet,
There is only
    One
    Loving
    The One
In another color, another form.
Oh, how beautiful are your eyes!
So unique in who you are,
Your quivering body
Presses against mine.

As we meet
In embrace and openness,
All else is lost.
I am speechless, and in awe.

"Me and you" has no meaning
In the place where we meet,
In such holy and natural
Union
As this.

WOUNDED

We are all marked
With wounds of this human life.

Soften and open.
It is not so bad
To taste
The blood of Christ.

Love heals
What cannot be made whole
By medicine
Of any other kind.

YES, THERE IS SUFFERING

Yes
Sweet angel,
It hurts:
A world at times so unkind,
Where Love is just a word.

Come.
I will hold your hand
And be with you
Inside the suffering
You endured so long
All alone.

Let me lay a warm mantle
Around your trembling heart,
For it is cold tonight.
We will lie inside
Each other's arms
And tuck our heads together
As birds tend to do.

Speak, dear one, wail.
Let it all fall to the ground.
I am here with you
Until the ache in your soul
Is emptied out
And peace fills the space

Between our hearts
And the starlit sky.

A simple Yes to suffering
Opens the door to compassion,
And we both are held, soft and warm,
In a heart big enough
For even the greatest pain
You have lived through.

THE BUDDHA SMILES

With a big smile,
I sit in this dream.
Nothing to change,
To run from, to figure out,
To fit the storyline,
To rise above into pink clouds,
Or to make up another drama
In the theater of life.

The Buddha is smiling,
And Maya keeps dancing on.
Dazzling beauty
Is emanating
From this one smile.
The heart is singing
A melody that no one
Ever has written,
Yet it is known
Throughout all time
And seen in all
Such smiles.

BEING HERE FOR YOU

Lean your tired head
Against my shoulder,
And I hold you
For a while, as only
A Mother will do.

With tender hands,
I stroke your hair,
Wipe your tears
From your precious face,
And give you a
Loving place to rest.

I won't bother you
With clever advice,
Fix you, or tell you
What you should do
"If I were you"—

But I will give you this:
To just receive all of you,
With all your bags
And treasures, too.

I am simply present,
Being here with you
As I gaze into your heart,
Which sighs in relief
To be met and held
As you are right now.

WHY?

Have you ever asked
This incessant question,
A word everyone is bothered by—
Why?
Where does it lead you?
An endless maze of answers
Trying to solve the Mystery
And so-called problems of life.

Crickets are chirping in concert
On a warm summer's night.
Why?
Soldiers are marching and killing
In another part of the world,
Why?
Children are crying with hunger,
Mothers are raped on the streets,
Why?
Lovers are embracing
In a sweet entanglement of kisses,
Why?
A grave is closing,
A friend gone from your side,
Why?
A great whale in the ocean
Gives birth to a new white calf,
Why?

A young man with a deadly disease
Gets up, miraculously recovered,
Why?
Two little girls playing hide and seek
Are hugging each other,
Why?

The mind scurries
To find a way to understand,
So that everything
Makes perfect sense.

Sweetheart, be still
In the midst of life's dance.
Revelation is here now,
In the silence where the wind doesn't blow,
And where Why does not even exist.

IF ONLY I COULD TELL YOU

If only I could tell you
That it is so worthwhile
To open your heart all the way.
For then you will love for real,
On that glorious, blessed day.

If only I could tell you
That it is fear that keeps you bound
In the delusions of mind
That makes you go round
Like a carousel.

If only I could tell you
That yes, your heart will break
A thousand times
From the joys and pains in life—
Oh, just let it!

If only I could tell you
That breaking the shell
Around your heart
Only frees you
To be who you really are,
Into living the fullness
Of love with us,

My friend!

*If only I could tell you
The place where you and I can meet . . .
Let us join here, today!*

GOD'S ORCHESTRA

God is making Love
To Love all the time!
What Universe have we landed on?
Rejoice!
Let's dance in this glory together.
Don't hold back, sweet one,
For we have only this moment,
And Love's orchestra
Is playing for us now!
Never mind
If one of us stumbles.
We give each other a hand
To get up again,
You don't need to do
Each step so perfectly.
Just have fun!
Come dance in the
Great ballroom of Life,
With all the lights on.
Don't let your Beloved one delight
In it all alone
When the music sings your tune.
Whirl and whirl
In the delirious joy of Love.
Forget that you ever did
Anything else.

HAPPINESS

Happiness sings a satiating melody
Beyond conditions that arise
And fly away.
Indian summer grasses sway
In gentle winds.
I am so contented,
Chewing berries in my hands.

Happiness finally arrived.
It never went anywhere.
The search for what
Was always here
Seems foolish, now,
And has ended.
The jewel is shining,
Simple and pure.
I cannot believe
I ever looked somewhere else
For the greatest gift—
Which is also bestowed upon you,
And is waiting to be realized.

*It is always with you,
In your own treasure chest.
You've got the key, dear friend!
Open to the diamond
In your heart, Beloved one,
And join the choir.*

*Chant with us
The song of true happiness
That has been singing in you
All along!*

FALLING IN LOVE

When you
Fall in Love
With your
Self
Without any condition
Of right and wrong
And all the other stuff
You've carried around so long,
The game of hide and seek
Is over—you're finally found—
And you arise,
Born anew.

From then on,
Love is freely
Living you,
And there is nothing
You can do about that anymore,
Only
Laugh
From your belly
Out loud
And wonder
Where you have been
All this time!

DON'T HOLD BACK LOVE

Don't hold back your Love.
It hurts every creature
When you dam up the river of Life.

You are fed by Love,
So feed others around you too,
Freely and generously
As Love is given to you.

What a joy for this earth
Is a woman or a man
Who lives like that.
Such rivers grow strong
And beautiful,
Flowing graciously
Back into the ocean,
To the Source
Where all rivers
Emerge from.

BEHOLD

Behold
In reverence
The treasure
Of a heart offered to you

Behold
In tenderness and care
The gift of a friend
Who is open and vulnerable with you

Behold
In respect
The presence of the only One
Who is really here with you

Behold
In wonder and awe
The beauty
Of another soul meeting you

Behold
In utter Love
The diamond
Of true Love given unto you

*Behold, my friend,
In gratitude,
This life as a gift
From God to you.*

LOVE IS

I am
Where all words fail
And silence just isn't enough.
Where all paths lead to
And no path enters here.
Where the fountain
In the garden of life
Stills all hunger and thirst.

A love so great
It contains all worlds.
A love so close
More intimate than my breath,
Smaller than fading dust in your hand.

A mighty river roaring through this body
Like the vast sky and warm earth
Deeper than the depth of the sea
Beyond the shores of knowing
Even evil and good.

All the way through,
One is human and divine.
In pure nakedness
Shine!

What is left you may ask?
Nothing.
Love is.

THE LOTUS GROWS
FROM THE MUD

Do you hear the whimpering, the crying
And howl from your prison inside?
Turn to what you have
Rejected, neglected,
Covered up and left out!

Like the leper
Ill, crippled, dying in a heap of trash.
The homeless
Filthy, disgusting to you're eye
Hungry and thirsty
For a single drop of love.
Like the chained, wounded dog
Ready to devour anyone
Who comes too near.
The ragged child
Frozen, unwanted,
Walking bare foot on ice
Reaching for a hand
In quiet despair.

The doors are guarded well
With the masks and armor you wear.
Hiding the terror deep down
And all what you have locked up
Inside yourself,

In the grand pursuit to survive this life.

What calls for you my dear?

Hear the agonizing scream
That pierces through
The wall of your soul!

For the sake of love
Dear one
Turn to that!

Face the unbearable pain
Without fixing, changing and avoiding
With yet another storyline.
Simply dare to open, soften
Into what scares you the most.

Meet the root of all suffering.
Allow your heart to break,
All the way trough
To the deepest darkest core!

I promise you
    Here
You are embraced
Beyond anything
You may have ever experienced
in your life

*By pure Love
Emerging from the ground
Of infinite Being.*

*That is, my dear
Your very own Self!*

*In the sacred place of mystery
You are awake
And realize in wonder
As all is turned around
From mud the lotus flower
Has grown and blooms*

In silent, radiant grace.

TRUE LOVE

Loves the whole of you
Yes,
Your hang ups and wrinkles too!
The soft radiance that shines
Through your beautiful eyes,
Your passionate kiss
And your soul's tenderness,
Your power and glory,
Dark secrets and folly mistakes
In this embrace
Nothing gets away!

True Love
Meets you just as you are
Here and now
In sheer grace
Beholds all of you
Never lets go
Even when you fall apart
Through the deepest wound in your heart
Surrender all the way
Into what you have been yearning for:
To be loved
Simply as you are.

*Precious One,
There is nothing to do,
True Love
Is always here for you!*

BE BRAVE

To truly love,
Open the chamber of your heart
Where all the secrets are contained.

Don't be so afraid to face
Your wounding and
All the "stuff"
You have carried around
Throughout your life.
Don't deny what's calling out to you
From the hidden dungeons of your soul!

All what you have been running from-
The shadow, the selfishness and pain-
Follows you every day.
Each time you turn away,
Each time you shut down
To your own heart and another one,
The dragon grows bigger then.

You think you feel safe,
Don't be deluded friend
You'll pay too high a price
And won't even be really alive!

The trail of blood
You leave behind

Will never give you peace
Until you set it right!
But choices made from ignorance,
Fear, and wounds
Can be healed my dear!

When you harm another,
You harm yourself.
When you love another,
You love your Self.
No difference, no separation,
Only one heart is here!

Remember, in the end
It is you who has to carry
The mountain of bags
That barricade the way
To your real lovingness.

Walk bravely through each gate,
No matter how terrifying
The demons look at the entrance, there.
Make your way to the other side,
Where a long lost pearl
Is waiting to be found.
You will get to the timeless shore
The longing to be home
Finally fulfilled!

Be brave, my love-
You are not alone.
We are all traveling through
This exquisite beauty and terrible mess
We are in this together my love!

Be brave!

NOBLE MAN

May I suggest:
When you meet
What is most vulnerable
And dear,
Never bring harm
Or do what may have been done
To you as a little and innocent one

Get on your knees, instead.
Put your armor down.
Serve Love
Like a noble man
By offering the only thing
That makes sense:
     Your heart!

Touch with tenderness.
Give respect and kindness.
Even if you have to sacrifice
Your pride and self-righteousness.
Dare to act greater than your fear,
For Truth has it's cost my dear!
Stand in the power of Love
Care from here!

Then, deer will come
To eat from your hand,

Birds will make a nest
Inside your head to rest,
And others will gladly
Snuggle close to you

Trustworthy and safe
You are a true refuge-

Noble at last!

THIS PAIN

Is ripping my chest
Over and over
With no end or ease in sight

This time
No story, no escape
No denial, no indulgence,
No transcendence
Nor even trying to heal.

I am done with all this.

This time
I open fully, all the way
To what is here now,
Simply as it is.

A flood of pain-
The agony, rage and sorrow too
Come rushing through
In a seeming never ending stream.
Blood is gushing from a rift inside.
My heart shatters
From this heavy rock
That burdened my whole life.

*Yet, what is in between?
What is left when all else fails?*

That, which softens and meets

I allow all as it is.

*Here, in the silence of breath
I find the ground beneath my feet.
My tears become healing rain,
Cleansing and bathing me
In the fountain of life.*

*I die into what is so
And fall through
Into what forever remains:*

*A Love so tender and immense,
I cannot name,
Springing forth from a well
That was buried deep inside.*

*This pain
Was the way
To Love
So true
And terribly wonderful.*

What emerges

Is the greatest gift:

This Love

Is you, me, and all.

It is.

ONE DROP

Only one drop
Of pure Love
Is the cure
That ends
The pain
Of an entire lifetime!

COME NEAR

So near
To the crashing of the waves,
The rhythm of the earth,
The twinkling of the stars,
The blooming flowers on the field,
To you Beloved One,
And the joy of being alive!

So near
To the despair of those unloved,
Cruel wars fought by minds gone insane,
Horrors committed
By those who do not know,
The homeless and starving for our greed,
To the one who has forgotten
And the pain we all experience too!

So near
In this heart
That is broken open
As wide as the world
With no answer but this:

*Come near
In love stand free
And meet all that is:
The horrible mess
And exquisite beauty
Of this human life as it is.*

*Come near
There is nothing to fear,
For in being fully here
-With a heart wide enough
To embrace the world as is-*

*We are joined together in a love
That lives each one of us!*

Come near!

THOU HAST KEPT THY PROMISE

Thou hast kept thy promise
Thou hast brought me home.

In my frenzy, insanity
And all things queer
I ran to and fro
Searching everywhere.

Exhausted from all roads taken
Betrayed and disillusioned too
I gave up and let go.
Surrendering into the wave
Of Thy mighty river,
Where all resistance melts down.

I can do no more
I die willingly into Thee,
Finally.

And then
In surprise
Amazing grace
Touches my tired face,
Sweeps me up into Thy embrace.

Revived
I taste the dew
Of fresh morning light
And arise!

In wonder and delight
In Thee I found my Self.
Love at last has captured me
And set me free
Into everlasting life!
Praised be Thee!

I AM

Give me no name,
I am called by many names:

I am human and divine,
I am Lover and Beloved.

I am the innocent child suckling
On the Mother's breast
I am the ever-giving Earth feeding freely
All creation.

I am the leaf wildly dancing
In the autumn winds
I am the snow silently covering winters ground
I am the first flower blossoming
In spring's renewal of life
I am the sunshine celebrating summers feast.

I am the river and the ocean
I am the rocks and the mountain
I am the stars and the sky
I am the volcano and the light bursting through.

I am the gentle tears upon your cheek
I am the Love inside your broken heart
I am the longing hands that lead you home.
I am the mystery on the threshold between

Worlds.
I am death and birth
I am all and none
I am shining and unchanging in the cycles of life.

I am the homeless starving on busy streets
I am the king proudly ruling the throne
I am the child playing in utter delight
I am the woman walking in sheer grace.

I am the doe and stag quietly grazing
Under the moonlight
I am the snake striking, devouring its prey
I am the owl hooting at midnight.

Dear one, see and hear-
Come here!

I am everlasting life
I am the love that forever is
I am the one with many names
I am no name, no word, bound by none

I am you blessed one
I AM!

THIS PRECIOUS EARTH

Soft wind cradles the air
Wild flowers blossom on the ground
Sweet milk flows from her bosom

This precious earth-
She feeds each creature abundantly
All life grows from her.
Pure waters stream from the mountaintop
To quench your thirst.
She gives fresh bread for the table
To still your hunger with.

Her beauty is all around,
Touching the eye of the beholder.
Birds sing praises to her
And rejoice in glorious sound.

This precious earth-
She offers all so graciously
Life blesses life continuously.
Honor her
Care for her
Love her
Share this gift!
She who gives and sustains your life
You are one with her!

DEATH IN AUTUMN

Forgotten memories emerge
Into the light of day
Past deeds pass bye
Emotions are stirred.

Leaves are falling
From a rain drenched sky.
Autumn has arrived,
Calling:" let go. Let go..."

How do you hold onto
A falling leaf
As if your life depends on it?

What dies
Is meant to die,
To change into another form,
To become compost
For tomorrow's flowers.
The rhythm of nature
Serves it's own creation.

What must die
Offers a last breath,
A sigh
Surrendering and returning

And finally

Graciously
Falling

Into the open hands
Of the infinite.

Let it.

WINTERSOLSTICE

The darkest night of the year is here
Stillness fills the air.
Deep down to the roots
Into the ground,
Sink.

Life breathes beneath frozen snow,
Weaving a quiet song.
Do you hear?
The tide is turning now,
The past is gone,
The new is ringing in.

Make a wish, dance and sing!
Celebrate the return of the sun
And let your beautiful light
Shine!

TO ALL WHO HAVE CLOSED DOWN

Oh, I know:
You have wanted to be invulnerable
And never experience hurt again.
So you built walls
Shut down,
And went numb.

This entire pretense
Is funny really,
And sad, actually.
When you look behind the walls and masks
Made by a terrified mind
In clever disguise
It is a defense
Meant to hide
Your precious human heart.

There is no pain, no joy, nor gain
In just being numb.
You may think you are safe
When you don't feel anything.
But everything has a price.

The trouble with this kind of survival
Is that you are deadening yourself.
In fear,
You aren't really alive.

In such a state,
Delusion comes easily, too.
For eyes
Which look at walls continuously
Don't see true-
Only shadows and plain fantasy.

When the doors are closed
And the pipes are blocked,
No love comes out or enters in.
Then it is easy to forget who you are,
To act noble or right
And happiness is plain out of sight.

You may be after god or enlightenment
By building your own firmament
To cover up your wrought-iron heart
In an attempt
To escape a world
That seems too scary and
Holds nothing for you.

You may wake up one fine day
In your self made prison cell
Desperately seeking the key to get out
While isolation creeps in like poison,
Where even bones get frozen
As you hunger in agony
For life, more than for bread.

You may still shrug your shoulders
And smirk,
"I don't care at all!"
Yet deep down
You can't deny
What is true:
The sting of deadly arrows
You have shot-
Arrows that cover the hardened ground
With the hot blood
Of those who came too close to you.

You may realize
When you face what is so
That you haven't really loved,
That your heart is empty
And your house ice cold
Isolated from all,
No loving word or touch
Coming through.

Wherever you are-
No matter how lost,
How huge your fort,
How many bombs lie hidden in your camp,
How many wrongs you've done,
How unworthy and terrified
Of love you feel you are-

Life is still pulsating from within
And will set you free
From all this insanity.

It takes only this:
The willingness to open
Is the key to live again.
Follow your deepest longing,
For it will lead you home.
Dare to act in integrity
For you live with what you do.
Allow yourself to be vulnerable,
To experience what is-
For it is your strength.

This is the way
Into your heart,
Where a treasure chest is waiting,
Glowing in the dark.
Here you will find
Pearls beyond price,
And in your deepest wound
Lies covered the precious gift
Of true love.

YOUR SONG

As the floodgates open
Joy, pain, anger and delight
All come dancing
Each to a different tune.
Wild, crazy, gentle and strong-
Until they hear
The steady rhythm of the drum
Played by the One
Who is at the center,
Where all music emanates from.

Yes, listen-
What wonder is this?
In its eternal sound
Is your soul's song!
Let the One direct your tune
And play in harmony
With the orchestra of life.
Courageously dance and sing
Your own melody!

The world needs you
As the trees need the sun
And the fields need the rain
To thrive.

YEARNING

What are you longing for
In the deepest recess of your soul?

Allow yourself to dive within.

And these burdens you have carried
Throughout your life,

Simply lay them down.

Just for now.

Come, be nourished and
Immerse in an ancient well,
Far too deep for words.

Drink from the water of life,

Even one drop
Quenches the thirsting ache in the chest.

Receive what you have been
Yearning for.

It is here

In your soul.

THE NAKED HEART

The naked heart
Is the gateway
Into Truth.

Nothing to defend or hide
Nowhere to go
Nothing to be or to do.

Touched by tears
And laughter, alike,
Simply alive,
And vulnerable,
As every human being
 Really is.

The heart unveiled
Is the eye of the needle
Into the great mystery
That pervades
And is
All life.

AN OFFERING

Listen to the forgotten song
Of your Being.

Follow all the way.
Your yearning takes you home
Into the deep dark
Where a brilliant light shines.

Don't stop short or sell out
Don't fear the shadows
Don't believe the lies-
Especially the nasty one:
That you have no worth.
Keep opening further than this
There is more my love.

Go to the end of the road
A gift is awaiting you-
To be received.

And then
With open hands to be given
As an offering
Into this world-

Calling your name.

I COME FOR YOU

I come for you,
As the lion roars
For the lamb.
The hawk circles in
On his prey,
Like the hunter
Shoots an arrow
Straight toward your heart.

I come for you
And I find you,
Be assured,
Like the wolf
Never looses
Track of his scent.

I come for you
Wearing many masks
To draw you closer in.
A dolphin playing
With the ocean wave,
The bear holding
Its furry cub,
Or the warrior
Lightning fire
Under your sweet butt.

I come for you
And stalk you
Silently,
As the panther
At night,
Until you have nowhere
To run or to hide.
I see you
With the eagle's eye.
The fierce lover
Is on his way
To swoop you up.

I come for you-
And when I am near,
I reveal my true face-
Which may shake you,
Trembling
Down onto the ground.

I come for you
And unveil you.
Fully naked
In your beauty
I will take you
Into an embrace

Where nothing but love
Will have a single chance
To survive.

Yes,

Count your days.

I am coming

For you, my dear!

I
    Am
        Coming
              For
                    You.

DON'T WAIT FOR LOVE

Don't wait for someone
To fall in love with.
Such only gives
A brief taste
From the feast
Prepared for you.

Before your very eyes,
Closer than your breath,
More intimate than
A kiss upon your lips,
Right here
In the flame
Of your own heart

Is the rose,
Which never fades.
Waiting for you
With the true promise
That cannot fail:

To forever live in love!

Don't wait Sweetheart.
Fall into love.
Feast now!

MY LOVE

I love you
And walk with you
All the way,
Wherever the path of life
Leads you through.
Whether you are riding high
On a magnificent horse,
Or laying low like a beggar
In the gutter,
I am with you.

I love you
And I see your beauty,
Even if you do not recognize yourself.
I meet you
In your tenderness,
Even when you try to appear tough.
I embrace you
In your grief and sadness,
Even if it is hard for you
To allow the darkness.
I hold you,
As you shake in fear,
Even when you would rather
Run or shut down.

I rejoice
In your wild passions and dreams,
Even if they have long been forgotten
In your soul.
I celebrate
Your talents and greatness,
Even though you may not believe
In yourself.

I love you
And kiss you
In all the places
That ache for loving touch.
I illumine
Your hidden secrets
And lift you up.

I dance
With the power of the God's
 Flowing through you
And take pleasure in you.
I bow to your compassion and awareness
And receive
Your precious gift of loving-kindness.
I hear you,
When you are silent,
When you sing praises or swear.
I feel your pain and joy
It is in my heart too.

I love you.
I break the chains that bind you
And set you free
To be really here.
I come at night
In surprise
To give to you
What you long for the most.
In daylight, at the appointed hour
I greet you
As my only Love.

I love you
As you are
All the way.
I am with you
Always.

I love you
And I live in you too, my dear.

WE

We curl into each other
Our worlds join
Where earth is meeting sky.

Our warm bodies dance
Sensuous and intimately
Reflecting the grace
Of a single rose
Unfolding
Into light.

We are drunk
With the ambrosia
That costs nothing,
But the offering
Of our whole hearts
Into love.

BELOVED

Your embrace shook the ground,
Your kiss turned my world around.
Your blazing fire set my heart alight
And burnt down my house.
Your wind swept through my life
And cleaned all closets out.
As the ocean you came to me,
Healed all wounds
And drowned me
In the glory of your love.

Your eyes see through
Into what is true.
Your smile is the sunlight in the day,
Your tears are rain pouring down,
Your strength gives shelter at night.
Your touch is pure ecstasy-
I can't get enough!
Your tenderness melts all hardness,
You move my heart
Stone by stone,
Falling open
I am home.

Beloved, you are the answer
To my prayer.
You are truly here
And never have let me down.
Lovingly you behold me,
As your most exquisite gift.
I receive you gratefully
As you enter slowly all the way.
My hands glide softly,
Caressing your luminous face
And joy floods my soul,
As the voice of passion
From deep within arises:

"Beloved, I love you with all my life!"

AN ANSWER TO THE WORLD'S SUFFERING

Hearts cry out
For justice and love!
Children starve
In the streets of Calcutta,
Women are raped
In homes of America,
Men die
In endless war.

Hands reach out
For compassionate action!
Whales breach
From the oceans pollution,
Animals disappear
Due to chemical destruction,
Our planet is poisoned
By our ignorance, greed and fear.

Life calls out
For awakening!
Don't succumb to denial and despair,
When you face the suffering that is here.
You do not need to save the word,
Feed all the hungry children,
End war forever,
Or clean up the entire mess

Single-handedly.
May I suggest:
Just get out there
And take a simple step.

Carry one fish into the ocean,
Smile at a stressed out cashier,
Offer your hand to a lost child,
Cook soup for someone hungry nearby,
Guide a thirsty soul to the well,
Pack your trash,
Love yourself enough,
Grow trees and wildflowers everywhere,
Speak and stand up
For that which you care!

Trust this revolution of the soul,
For every loving act affects the whole!

Sweetheart,
Don't mind getting your hands dirty,
As we all do
In the labor of life and death.
Don't mind the breaking of your heart
As it must,
When you truly love.
Don't mind waking up from the slumber
In this world
And taking your part!

*Blessed one,
Let your answer be this:
Shine your light
For one more
Makes the world a brighter home.*

*Take every moment
For you have only this one
As a precious chance to love.*

*Most of all, my angel,
Remember your wings
And spread beauty wherever you are.*

*What greater power is there
When our hearts and hands
Are joined in love
And dare to act together
For the benefit of all,
My dear?*

SHE

Awaken,
You have entered sacred ground!
Magic fills the air,
The Goddess is here!

Turn around,
Creatures of every kind
Flock to her.
People come to her-
Some in fear,
Others worship her-
It does not matter to her.
With her power
She embraces all-
The singing and the weeping,
The blood and the blossoms-
In her great, tender heart.

Her touch makes trees quiver,
Her kiss gives life to a dying soul.
Her beauty, which time can't destroy,
Captures the beholders eye.
She dances in ecstasy
With the waves of the ancient sea.
She walks graciously
Through the hard mountains
And the soft earth.

*She rests in stillness,
As her body moves with the wind.
Her song is of light,
Falling through darkness
Like a shooting star.*

*She takes and gives
Without asking you.
With a caring hand
She nourishes a newborn baby,
With one stroke
Takes back another
And licks the bones of those decayed.*

*She creates the stars
And the earth you stand upon,
Always changing form.
Do not cling or resist,
But live with her.
You may cry and laugh,
Just remember-
It is Love
That always stays and is.*

*Hers is not a religion
Of do's and don'ts,
Her hair is too wild for such.*

Life and death
Is her breath.
She holds this world,
And you as well,
In her infinite hands.

She, who is,
Blesses you.
Only one Teaching
She offers to you:

Let love live you,
For the sake
Of all that is.

DOWN FROM THE THRONE

Let's take love down
From the holy throne
Of lofty ideals and conditions
That no one seems
To fulfill anyway.

Let's take love down
To you and me.
The moment
In between
Two hands touching
And one heartbeat.
Here is where we meet.

Let's take love down
And wrestle wildly,
Play hide and seek,
Laugh and cry together.
And share our
Longing and joy.

Let's take love down,
And meet each other

As we really are.

So love can breathe and fully LIVE.

AMORE TE - LET ME LOVE YOU

Let me kiss you awake
From your slumber.
Let me carry you
Into the soft radiance of Light
And whisper a secret,
The only one you and I
And the whole world shall know:
"Beloved, you are precious as you are."

Everything else they told you,
In an insane world like this,
Was just a big fat lie
That led you,
Like so many of us,
Astray.

Let me love you all the way
Just as you have been yearning for.
Whilst so often others,
Feeling separate,
Have looked out for themselves, alone.
Let me tell you,
As I hold the palm of your hand,
The one truth I have found
At the core of all creation:

There is nothing but Love, here.

May I suggest, beautiful one,

Simply surrender

Into THAT!

EPILOGUE

This is the beginning
And the end
Of our journey
And all the poems
I had the exquisite pleasure
Of sharing with you—
THAT which you already
Know in your heart—
Which has woven
The golden thread
Between us
That connects all
Across the world,
In nothing
But Love.

May you be blessed
And enjoy your life!

With all my love,
Nicola.

ABOUT THE AUTHOR:

Dr. Nicola Amadora is a mother, writer, speaker and works as a Psychologist, Women's Leadership and Relationship Trainer, and Spiritual Teacher. She offers private sessions and teaches internationally by invitation.

To contact her please visit:
www.nicolaamadora.com

"Kissed by Fire" her second book will be released in 2014. A book to inspire real love for people, the earth and you. It is a unique symphony of true-life stories, practical skills and mystical wisdom teachings. Look for it!

And keep looking for the treasure right at your feet, even in the mud there is a glimmer. Share some love along your walk, it lights up the world. I hope this book gave you a taste: "You are loved, just as you are".

Printed in Great Britain
by Amazon